Trains

Disney Monorail

by Julie Murray

2

Dash!
LEVELED READERS
An Imprint of Abdo Zoom • abdobooks.com

Dash!
LEVELED READERS

Level 1 – Beginning
Short and simple sentences with familiar words or patterns for children who are beginning to understand how letters and sounds go together.

Level 2 – Emerging
Longer words and sentences with more complex language patterns for readers who are practicing common words and letter sounds.

Level 3 – Transitional
More developed language and vocabulary for readers who are becoming more independent.

THIS BOOK CONTAINS
RECYCLED MATERIALS

abdobooks.com

Published by Abdo Zoom, a division of ABDO, PO Box 398166, Minneapolis, Minnesota 55439.
Copyright © 2022 by Abdo Consulting Group, Inc. International copyrights reserved in all countries.
No part of this book may be reproduced in any form without written permission from the publisher.
Dash!™ is a trademark and logo of Abdo Zoom.

Printed in the United States of America, North Mankato, Minnesota.
102021
012022

Photo Credits: Alamy, Getty Images, iStock, Shutterstock
Production Contributors: Kenny Abdo, Jennie Forsberg, Grace Hansen, John Hansen
Design Contributors: Candice Keimig, Neil Klinepier, Victoria Bates

Library of Congress Control Number: 2021940211

Publisher's Cataloging in Publication Data

Names: Murray, Julie, author.
Title: Disney monorail / by Julie Murray
Description: Minneapolis, Minnesota : Abdo Zoom, 2022 | Series: Trains | Includes online resources and
    index.
Identifiers: ISBN 9781098226718 (lib. bdg.) | ISBN 9781644947234 (pbk.) | ISBN 9781098227555
    (ebook) | ISBN 9781098227975 (Read-to-Me ebook)
Subjects: LCSH: Monorail railroads--Juvenile literature. | California--Disneyland--Juvenile literature. |
    Disney, Walt, 1901-1966--Juvenile literature. | Visionary architecture--Juvenile literature. | Railroad
    travel--Juvenile literature.
Classification: DDC 388.42--dc23

Table of Contents

Disney Monorail

The Disney Monorail **System** is known as the "highway in the sky"!

5

The first **monorail** opened at California's Disneyland in 1959. It is used to get around the park. Riders also take in great views!

The Tokyo Disney **monorail** opened in 2001. Its windows are shaped like Mickey Mouse's head!

Over the years, some of the trains have had fun movie themes.

Disneyland was ready for Pixar Fest in 2018. The blue train featured *Finding Nemo* characters. The Incredible family was on the orange train!

Walt Disney World Monorail

The **monorail** at Walt Disney World in Orlando, Florida, opened in 1971.

The **monorail** has three different **lines** that connect six stations in the parks and hotels.

Do Not Enter

15

There are 12 trains in the **system**. Each one has a different colored stripe.

Each train has six **cars**. About 360 people can ride each train at once.

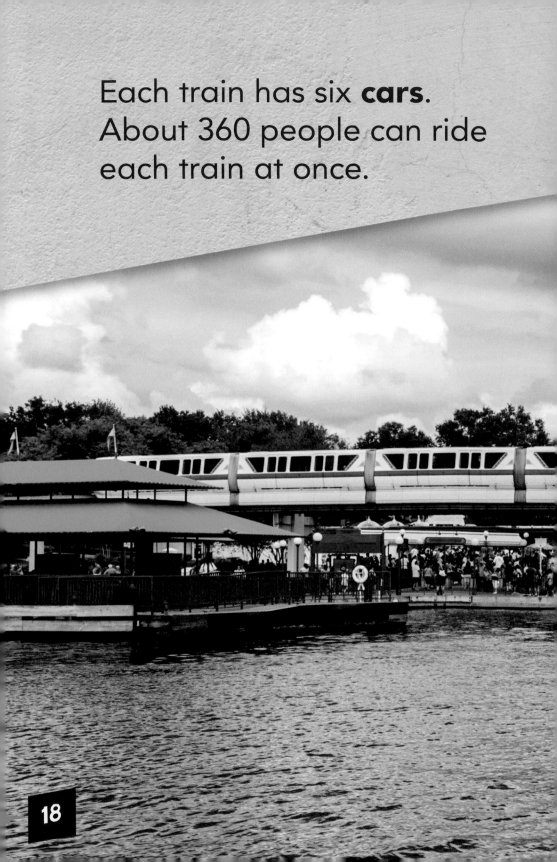

The **monorail** at Walt Disney World is one of the most used in the world! About 150,000 people ride it each day.

More Facts

- The Walt Disney World Monorail **System** has 14.7 miles (24 km) of track.

- Each train's top speed is 55 mph (89 kph).

- The trains run on their own and are on a schedule. Still, pilots sit in each train in case of an emergency.

Glossary

car – a vehicle that runs along rails, such as a railroad car or cable car.

line – one of the many different lines, or railway, in a train system. Lines can be different sizes and serve different people. Some lines allow trains to move faster than others.

monorail – a railroad whose cars run along a single rail, or the rail itself.

system – a group of parts that work together as a whole.

Index

Online Resources

Booklinks
NONFICTION NETWORK
FREE! ONLINE NONFICTION RESOURCES

To learn more about the Disney Monorail, please visit **abdobooklinks.com** or scan this QR code. These links are routinely monitored and updated to provide the most current information available.